Johnston Hale
PUBLICATIONS

Heartfelt

A collection of poems written
from the heart

Joanne Boyle

Designed by
Celia J-Hale

Produced by
Johnston-Hale Publications
in the United Kingdom
2022

www.johnston-hale.co.uk

Issue 1

Author Joanne Boyle

Johnston-Hale
PUBLICATIONS

Foreword:

As a little girl I would sit in the library reading fairy tales and looking at all the colourful pictures. Growing up nothing has changed, but now I take photographs that inspire me to write about anything from magic to mental health.

I try to put a different picture in people's minds to enable them to look at things from a different view. This book has been a dream for so long...and it is now my legacy.

Joanne xxx

This book is dedicated to my Family.

They are my inspiration behind every heartfelt emotion. The poem dancing with memories was inspired by us all walking on a beach on a cold winter morning.

They are my everything.

To Nicola, Craig, James, Grayson and Tilly, the sun never goes down when you are around.

To my Husband and my best friend, the man that taught me how unselfish true love is, I thank you and love you. xxx

I don't need my eyes to see you

I don't need my eyes to see you.
They don't enable me to live.
I just need a heart to feel,
to teach me how to give.

I don't need to look to see you.
Or touch to know you are there.
Whatever I have in my hand,
I will give to all to share.

I don't need to see the footsteps,
that surround me in the sand.
It doesn't matter who you are,
I shall offer you my hand.

I don't need my eyes to paint,
all these pictures in my mind.
All I need is love, in,
every paintbrush that I find.

My pallet is very vibrant.
Nothing is black and white.
I don't need my eyes to see you,
or to paint a world that's bright.

Snowman

Once I met a snowman, with a smile upon his face.
He never seemed to move, from the same old place.

I asked why he was smiling. Why he didn't go to bed?
He looked at me with button eyes and this is what he said:

I watch the people dashing by. They never stop to chat,
but occasionally a child will try to take my hat.

This always makes me smile. It means that I am seen.
I am still a part of Christmas and not of one that's been.

I love to watch the children, to hear them laugh and play.
I love to be a memory, to be a part of Christmas day.

So this is why I smile, as I stand outside this door.
I am part of a tradition and I want for nothing more.

The little girl touched him, she felt he was stone cold
She knew he was alive though from the story he had told.

She now had a friend and knew one day he would melt.
She would never forget, the snowman she had felt.

Homeless

When the days are cold,
and night times turn to frost.
When beds are made from cardboard,
and people's homes are lost.

When everything that matters,
just tucks up in a sack.
When everything you own,
gets carried on your back.

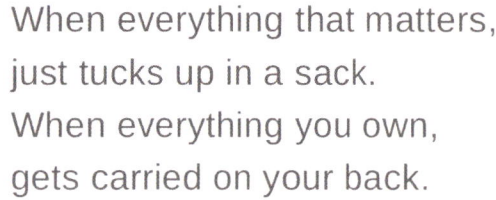

When the wind chills your ears,
you wear a hood upon your head.
Walk toward the light,
before you make your bed.

So many people are homeless,
as day turns into night.
When hearts are filled with dread,
there is no hope in sight.

Cherish the roof above you.
The logs upon your fire.
The family that you fight with,
is for someone else to desire.

Christmas is for giving,
but so is every day.
Give kindness to those who need
it.
Throw that receipt away.

Friendship's Whisper

I thought of you today.
I realised it had been a while,
since we had a catch-up,
so I got my phone to dial.

Then I got distracted.
The days then turned to weeks.
Are we really friends?
When friendship hardly speaks.

Yet in our hearts we know,
the love is always there.
When one of us needs the other
we are there to care.

Friendship has a whisper.
It doesn't go unheard.
It wraps you in its love, and
it is forever shared.

EDDY

We walked so many walks.
Together just you and I.
We didn't care about the weather.
We just let the day pass by.

You would give me lots of treats,
but the biggest treat was you.
You said I was your best friend,
you were my best friend too.

Together we would walk for miles.
Sometimes I would run and play.
I knew you loved those moments,
so remember me that way.

I know that you still miss me.
I am still by your side.
Still wagging my tail like always,
as I walk with you with pride.

Heaven...

With each Memory take a step toward,
the light that shines on you.
In the distance are the shadows,
of those that you once knew.

You can hear your Mother calling.
She has waited for so long.
She has missed her Cinderella,
since the day that she had gone.

Your Father holds his arms out,
he waits to hear you sing.
He has missed your entertainment,
he said it was your thing.

Your eldest boy is sitting,
he wants to see his Mum again.
He looks so handsome in his attire,
now he is free from pain.

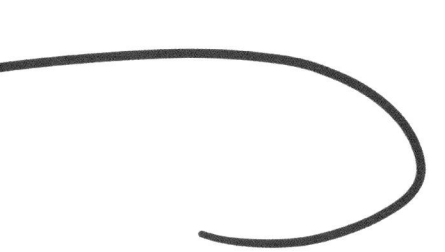

Your Daughter sits with her Husband,
she is on her Daddy's knee.
They are waiting for you to join them,
to rejoice in Family.

Our Christopher has you flowers,
just like he did before,
but this time he stands waiting,
in the arch of Heaven's door.

So many brothers and sisters,
and friends from times gone by.
Just follow the light sweet angel.
Spread your wings and fly.

Are you home yet Nana?
In the company of all those gone?
Do you hear Madame Butterfly?
Do they sing your favourite song?

Are you smiling Nana?
In the arms of those you love.
You left this world behind you,
to join the one above.

...is waiting

Nana Mondays

I would wake up on a Monday Morning,
wondering what to wear.
Being careful with my make-up,
and how I did my hair.

I would then go and do the shopping.
I had a list that I would check twice.
I would search for firm tomatoes,
and would always check the price.

I learnt how to squeeze a loaf of bread,
and which shampoo not to buy.
How chocolate biscuits had been shrunk,
and the difference of an apple pie.

When you asked for a cream sponge,
I searched for one that colour. (haha)
I came back with a blue one,
and oh we laughed for sure.

I knew one day I would cherish,
every memory that we made,
and that I would miss my Nana Mondays
but my memories wouldn't fade.

Depresssion

You woke me up this morning,
just so you could see.
The person beneath the eyes,
wasn't really me.

You made me look outside,
though it was so bleak.
You said there was always tomorrow.
You had said the same all week.

You pushed me back to bed.
You said you'd take care of it all.
You told me if I slept,
it would save me from a fall.

You told me not to eat.
That in time I would be thin.
You understood my mind.
You felt me from within.

"You spoke about
tomOrrow..."

You spoke about tomorrow.
All that we would do.
I knew it was a lie,
though I tried to believe in you.

You said you'd mind the kids.
That you would watch them play.
You said they didn't need me.
They were better off this way.

I thought you were my friend.
I gave you all my trust.
Admittedly I gave it easy.
I saw it as a must.

Then I heard you talking.
You were whispering my name.
I heard you say I had given up,
that my life was not the same.

These words pricked my conscience,
although the prick was small.
I got out of bed the next morning,
pushed against that wall.

I looked outside the window.
I saw a different view.
I felt a glimmer of hope,
I knew what I had to do.

I called upon a person.
I did not care just who.
My life deserved a purpose,
I just had to make it through.

Baby Whisper

For every kiss we can never give you.
For every smile we will never see.
For every step we never saw you take,
you are still part of our family.

For all the toys we never bought you.
For every tantrum you never took.
For every adventure we never went on,
you are still a memory in our book.

For every Christmas you are not here.
For every gift we did not buy.
For all the cuddles we can not give you,
we send kisses to the sky.

For every birthday there is no cake.
For all the candles we can not light,
we shall look up to the clouds and
see our Angel shining Bright.

For every feeling in our hearts.
For every breath you did not take,
you will always be so very loved and
be part of every memory that we make.

Mammy & Daddy

xxx

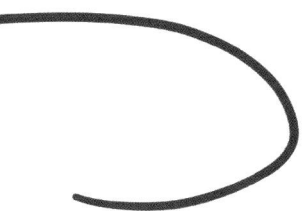

I am sorry I could not stay with you,
this is not what God had planned.
He knew you would take care of me,
and forever hold my hand.

He realised I was still needed though,
and I did not question why?
I just put my Angle wings back on,
and flew back to the sky.

I turned and waved goodbye
when the time came to depart.
I left a kiss upon your cheeks,
and my footprint in your heart.

I wish I could have stayed longer,
but it was not meant to be.
I know that I was wanted,
and how much you both loved me.

I shall sit upon my cloud in heaven,
and watch you from above.
I will blow away your tears,
and fill your hearts with love.

Kisses from Heaven
Baby Whisper

xxx

Tell me you love me, just one more time.
Rock me to sleep, singing a Nursery rhyme.
Come and play hide and seek with me.
Don't say I am too big to sit on your knee.

Count my fingers and my ten toes.
Pretend to pinch my button nose.
Shout out loud, where are you?
Knowing fine well, you can see my shoe,

Just one more time, hold my hand,
Comb my hair with every strand.
Wash my face and behind my ears.
Be my hope and not my fears.

Just one more time let me be small.
Pick me up when you see me fall.
Just one more day, before we grow old,
and time becomes a tale of a story told.

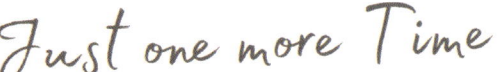

Just one more Time

Voice

I have a voice inside my head.
It dare not speak for fear or dread.
It screams and shouts but no one hears.
So my day continues with silent fears.
Your voice is heard through silent words.
You are here because we cared.
You need to know you're not alone,
just reach out and use that phone.

My bed has a voice that beckons me.
It keeps me safe from reality.
The blankets are the friends I wish I had.
The stench a reminder I was bad.
We are your friends. We won't go away.
We will be your voice every day.
The bed will be for you to rest,
let us help, we know what's best.

Food is the enemy to make me fat,
It thinks I don't know where it is at.
I will flush it away if it comes near me.
I am in control of my own body.
Food is the fuel you need to live.
Little by little, we will give
until you see your pretty little face.
You are amongst friends in this place.

I can feel these chains, dragging me down.
My thoughts are the flood in which I'll drown.
This life is somewhere I don't belong.
I'm done with it, I want it gone.
We have the key to unlock those chains.
We have the love to pick your brains.
We have the voice to speak for you.
We will be your voice if you ask us to.

Once upon a time,
where magic has no end.
A place hatred doesn't love, and
everyone's your friend.

Where prince charming was born,
and money grows on trees.
Where frogs are loved for minds,
our worth is found in peas.

Where ducklings become swans.
From believing in one's self.
Tom thumb and Thumbelina,
are not left upon the shelf.

The Emperor was not scorned upon,
for the clothes he did not wear.
Rapunzel's tower was her palace,
her ladders were her hair.

Jack that loved his Mother,
still walks the streets today.
Gulliver goes on his travels,
a new adventure every day.

Mrs Heartfelt lived a dream,
to always give a smile.
To remember that a life,
is to make it all worthwhile.

Once
Upon a
Time

Today I made a wish

Today I made a wish,
for all the world to hear.
I wished for children to play,
without living in fear.
I wished to see my Nana,
to sit on Granda's knee.
I wished to play hide and seek,
I wished to run free.
I wished I could walk to school,
to run and greet my friend.
I wished to play a game of tag,
I wished for covid to end.
Today I made a wish, and
I know it will come true, because
dandelions are fairies,
and they make sure that they do,

Halloween Turnip

When I was a little girl.
I would spend hours with a spoon,
cutting out a turnip,
trying to make its shape a moon.

My Mam would cut two holes,
make a handle from a string.
We would wear a bin bag with
a hole that was cut in.

Mam would light us a candle.
No tea lights existed then.
We would use melted wax,
it stuck on the count of ten.

The wind was always blowing,
the candle never stayed lit.
The evening was still loved though,
every single bit.

We went knocking on the doors,
singing a little song.
Not everyone would answer
or leave their lights turned on.

We had butterflies in our tummies.
No pot to collect sweets.
We were lucky to get pennies
still, we walked the streets.

Those days are in the past.
They have brought us to today.
A time when children dance
in the memories we replay.

Mental Health

When you think nobody cares how broken you are,
or you think they can't understand.
When even the outside feels too small,
and you no longer want a hand.

When the sky feels like it's suffocating,
and the ground hurts your feet.
When the smile becomes a fake hello,
to the people that you greet

When the reasons don't matter anymore,
and there's nothing left to give.
When the empty hole,
is where you want to live.

When everyone around you,
becomes invisible to your eye.
When you are drained of emotion
with no tears left to cry.

When love can no longer save you,
you are in the depths of despair
You have gone deaf to all the voices
that scream "hang on" in there.

Yet the world is still uneducated,
no one knows just what to do.
If love and listening were enough,
then it would have saved you.

The Christmas Angel

I kissed you on the forehead,
whispered in your ear.
Did you feel me touch your cheek,
as I wiped away a tear.
I helped you out of bed,
I will help you face the day.
Do not dwell on Christmas Past,
I never went away.
Sit beside the Christmas tree,
feel my presence near.
Sing our favourite carols,
soon I shall appear.
Laugh at all the cracker jokes,
let them bring you joy.
Remember all the magic,
for every girl and boy.
Eat your Christmas dinner,
and pull me up a chair.
You do not need to see me,
but I will still be there.

Generations

Over six decades and seven years,
I was a boy like you.
I did not have that many toys,
we were lucky to have a shoe.

My Father was a fisherman.
He went out on a boat.
He earned a living selling fish,
to keep us all afloat.

We didn't have a television.
We just went out to play.
The streets were always full of kids.
It was good back in the day.

I have lived to see changes,
though some I don't like.
When I was seven,
I was out riding my bike.

One thing that remains
that age can never falter.
The love between a Family,
generations can not alter.

Don't Give Up

Don't give up on the morning sun,
or forget that it is there.
Don't give up on the blowing wind,
or when the raindrops wet your hair.
Don't give up on the moment,
because of something that you feel.
Don't give up on the laughter
after all, those times were real.
Don't give up on the life,
the one you are blessed to live.
Don't give up on the love,
you still have more to give.
Don't give up on the Family,
let them be your crutch.
Don't give up on hope,
you are loved so very much.
Don't give up on daylight.
Let it light your way.
Don't give up on tomorrow,
because of yesterday.

TO:

My Younger Self

Don't ever be invisible, or forget to wear that smile.
Don't care what others think, keep being versatile.

Always be the light, to someone else's dark.
Always be the ignition, to someone else's spark.

Breathe in every season. Love the sun and rain.
Trample on the leaves then trample on them again.

Jump in every puddle. Slide along the ice.
Hop on every paving stone, in fact, hop on them twice.

Dance with all you've got. Be whom you want to meet.
Play hide and seek with friends, and hopscotch in the street.

Open your mind to adventures. Don't be ruled by fear.
Don't be afraid to love and welcome every tear.

Always look for the positives and the positives you'll find
But most importantly of all, don't ever stop being kind.

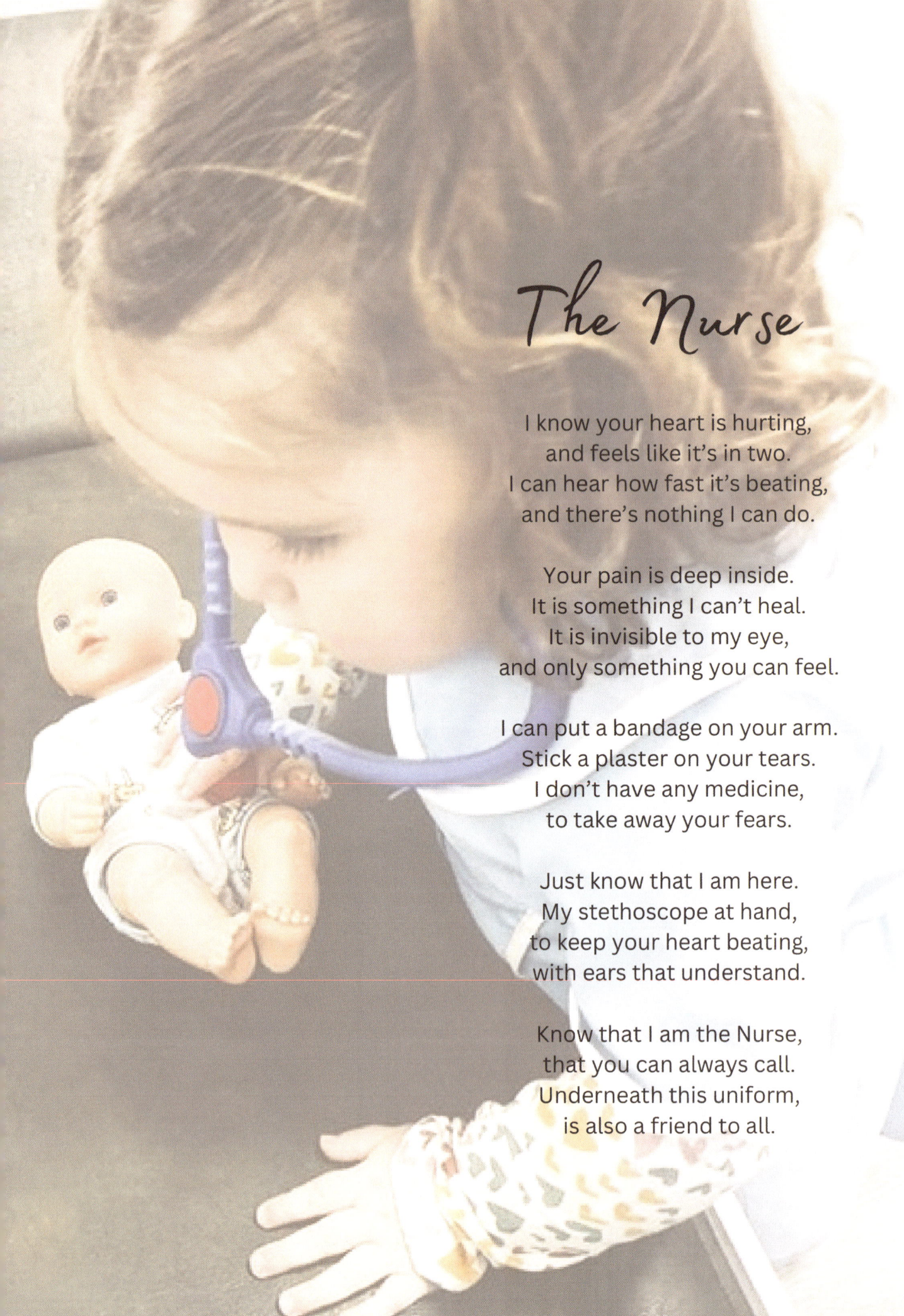

The Nurse

I know your heart is hurting,
and feels like it's in two.
I can hear how fast it's beating,
and there's nothing I can do.

Your pain is deep inside.
It is something I can't heal.
It is invisible to my eye,
and only something you can feel.

I can put a bandage on your arm.
Stick a plaster on your tears.
I don't have any medicine,
to take away your fears.

Just know that I am here.
My stethoscope at hand,
to keep your heart beating,
with ears that understand.

Know that I am the Nurse,
that you can always call.
Underneath this uniform,
is also a friend to all.

Dance
with
me
Brother

Dance with me Brother,
before we grow old.
Let us make ripples,
splash in the cold.

Jump with me Brother,
whilst we still are young.
Let us get wet.
Let us have fun.

Hold my hand Brother.
Let us play together.
Let us make a memory,
to cherish forever.

Skip with me Brother.
Show me the way.
Let us live in the moment,
of the world of play.

Christmas Spirit

I kissed you on the forehead.
Whispered Happy Christmas in your ear.
Did you feel me touch your cheek,
as I wiped a tear?

I will help you out of bed.
I will help you face the day.
Do not dwell on Christmas past,
I never went away.

Sit beside the Christmas Tree.
Feel my presence near.
Sing our favourite carols,
soon I will appear.

Laugh at all the cracker jokes,
let them bring you joy.
Remember all the magic,
for every girl and boy.

When you eat your Christmas lunch,
pull me up a chair.
You do not need to see me,
to know that I am there.

Christmas Card

I wrote you out a Christmas card,
I filled it full of love.
I used my tears to seal it,
then I addressed it to Above.

I put it in a pillar box.
I hope it finds it's way,
but just in case it doesn't,
this is what I want to say:

I hope that up in heaven,
there is a Christmas tree.
And the Angel on the top
is you looking down on me.

I hope you are singing carols,
and Dancing in the sky.
I hope you catch my kisses,
I blew them way up high.

I'll think of happy memories,
the gift you left behind.
The gift of Christmas love
is the greatest gift to find.

Follow me Sister.
Let me lead the way.
Life has many stepping stones,
that get bigger every day.

The trick is to be cautious,
to use your judgement well.
Don't ever look behind you,
even if you fell.

Always keep going forward.
You will get there in the end.
Each stone is a chapter,
of a story with no end.

So stay behind me Sister.
Let me lead the way.
One day you won't follow, and
I shall long for yesterday.

Follow me Sister

It's a Dog's Life

I'll wake up on a morning,
after sleeping in your bed.
I try to get your attention,
by sitting on your head.
I want to go outside,
will you open up the door?
I want to do my business,
you already know what for.
I will not rest until you get up.
I am ready for my feed.
After we shall go walking,
I will fetch my lead.
I wag my tail profusely.
You know just how I feel.
Where is my squeaky toy?
Let's play hide and steal.
My bark is the voice I use,
that tells you "I love you"
I will be your best friend,
loyal and forever true.

The first Christmas

Ten little fingers. Ten little toes.
A mop of hair. A Cute button nose.

A gift of love, to bring us joy.
A beautiful baby, girl or a boy.

Magical moments, for all to remember.
The first Christmas. The first December.

A pair of booties, and a baby grow.
Warm fairy lights. The very first snow.
A Christmas bauble, on a Christmas tree.
The greatest gift, called a Family.

It doesn't come wrapped, in a shiny bow.
It just follows you, wherever you go.

Believe

With Christmas comes a story,
a one that's seldom told.
The secret of its meaning,
was bought with a bag of gold.

The magic was forgotten,
and Santa shook his head.
He looked across at Rudolph,
his nose was no longer red.

He thought of giving up.
He was feeling weak.
He held on to a candy cane,
in the hope that strength he'd seek.

As one candy cane helped him,
he found greater strength in two.
He then called upon his elves,
after all he had a few.

The elves all got together, and
the reindeer came around.
Rudolph's nose was red again,
believing was now found.

They sprinkled a little stardust,
a bit for every girl and boy, and
Santa whispered Thank you,
on the return of Christmas joy.

Autism

That Chocolate bar you gave me, that was broken into three.
The one that made me cry, because they weren't cut equally.

Those stairs you walked down first, as I walked behind!
The ones that made me cry, because I like going first you'll find.

The Breakfast that you gave me, with my spoon of chocolate
spread, I am sorry that I cried, for the way you cut my bread.

Those chicken nuggets that I love, weren't cooked just right today.
I am sorry that I cried, I can't help being this way.

I know I make things hard for you, but I don't know how to change.
I am sorry that I cried, for all that I find strange.

You see I have my ways, and I know they frustrate you.
I am sorry that I cried, but I get frustrated too.

You see I am made different, it'd hard to understand.
I have heard it is called Autism and I need a helping hand.
To me it's all I know, and all I ask of you,
is to please try to see it from my point of view.

I don't do things to be naughty, or want to spoil your day.
I just don't know how to be any other way.

The twinkle

Together we sat and laughed,
under the lights of the Christmas tree.
Six of us in our Family,
a sex of two times three.
We spoke about our lives,
laughed at memories shared.
We no longer cared about the gifts,
we were there because we cared.
We spoke of Yesteryear, and
as we sat and listened.
We saw in our reflections,
that our eyes now glistened.
We were the children of our time,
from memories left behind.
If only we could go back there,
I wonder what we'd find.
Underneath that Christmas tree,
with its sparkle and all its shine,
was the greatest gift of all,
in a Family that is mine.

Fairy Godmother

I had a Magic wand,
it shone a shining light.
It helped to lead the way,
to those that are lost at night.

It lit up a little corner,
but enough to see ahead.
I hoped my magic wand,
would help to ease their dread.

I showed them a direction.
I prayed that they would see.
I was their Fairy Godmother,
I prayed they'd follow me.

I will walk with you.
I'll never leave your side.
Not until you are ready,
to want to no longer hide.

Be someone else's light.
The magic in their day.
Be the friend that you want,
and help them find their way.

Close your eyes Mama

Close your eyes Mama, say goodbye to the day.
Close your ears to the world, and all it has to say.
Let your heart rest. Let the pain go.
Rest all your limbs, stop saying no.

Close your eyes dear Wife, as I hold your hand.
In sickness and in health, our vows still stand.
Dance to the clouds. Sing our favourite song.
The Angels will be waiting, don't keep them long.

Close your eyes Nana, as we sing lullabies
like you sang to us when you heard our cries.
We will rock you to heaven, where the Angels await.
We will only leave you at heaven's gate.

Close your eyes dear friend, that has touched our life.
You were the perfect Mother, Nana and Wife.
We will never forget or stop loving you.
Our loss is heavens Gain of an Angel so true.

Remembrance

My Father shook my hand. I heard my Mother cry.
I had to go to fight, but I was afraid that I may die.
I was just a boy. I didn't want to go to war.
I wanted to stay home but duty was called for.

I was needed to help my country, along with many others.
We had to fight for freedom, for Sisters and our Brothers.
My heart was beating fast. At times it was all I heard.
I had a job to do, no time for feeling scared.

I would sit deep in a trench, all faces looked the same.
Hiding beneath the dirt, not knowing no one's name.
The enemy would attack. I could see my Mother's face.
I knew I had to fight, to make the world a better place.

I got to see my Mum again and Dad didn't shake my hand.
He pulled me to his chest, which helped me to understand.
I fought to save our country and I would do it all again.
Thousands did not make it, but they didn't die in vain.

Now we live in freedom. We get to see our Families grow.
The children are our future, because of wars sorrow.
Thank you to all the parents who lost their loving Sons.
They all died heroes at the cost of others' guns.

Walk with me

Come and walk with me,
you don't need to speak.
Just know I am here,
at times you feel weak.

Come walk with me,
I shall take your pace.
Let us breathe in the air.
Let us have some space.

Come walk with me,
I shall take your stride.
One step at a time,
the berth is wide.

Come walk with me.
We are best friends.
We will be that way,
until our journey ends.

The Care Assistant

I came into your home today,
in fact, I came in twice.
Each time I introduced myself,
that is dementia's price.
I spoke about the weather,
knowing you would forget.
I knew you would remember,
the lady that you met.
We sat and watched TV.
Laughed at things we said.
We sang a few songs
before you asked to go to bed.
Each time I left the room,
just went behind a door.
The illness would take hold again,
and I'd introduce myself once more.
To you, I am a stranger,
every time we meet.
To me, you are my Lady,
so lovely and so sweet.

The Cup of Tears

I woke up from my sleep this morning, I did not want to do.
My days are nothing but nightmares, I don't want to make it through.

I make myself a coffee. I look out to the sky.
The cup now fills with tears, in fact it never runs dry.

I go back in my mind, and relive the times we shared.
I try to fill this empty hole, by grasping memories spared.

The hole can not be filled though. I don't know how to live.
Tomorrow shall be the same, as I have nothing more to give.

I search everywhere for answers, knowing there's none to find.
I long to close my eyes again. To put darkness in my mind.

I walk the streets of ignorance. My loss is their unknown.
I look upon all children, as I cry for the loss of my own.

I have to go on living though, with this great big empty space.
It represents my love for you. As my heart id does replace.

Anorexia

The Friend

You didn't see me standing there,
as I watched you from the side.
I admired all your beauty,
which you feel you need to hide.
You did not hear me tell you,
just how loved you are.
You did not see my eyes,
twinkle like a star.
You did not want to know,
what your self-worth is all about.
You clearly blocked your ears,
so you couldn't hear me shout.
So I grabbed my arms around you,
I screamed just look at me.
Walk away from the girl in the mirror,
it is time to set her free.
Go and dazzle with your smile,
show your beauty from inside.
Next time you see that girl,
look at her with pride.

The Enemy

When I look in the mirror
and see her staring back at me.
It makes me feel so worthless,
because of what I see.
In front of me is an image,
it is not a pretty sight, and
then the enemy takes hold,
I then find it hard to fight.
So I listen to the lies,
believe everything I hear.
Food becomes the poison.
Moments become fear.
The Family that I love,
are now invisible to my eyes.
My only focus now
is to claim the enemy's prize.
Every day I wake up thinking,
about her staring back at me.
One day I hope to look,
and see her as being pretty.

My home is my Kingdom,
which I see in my mind.
It is a place that no path,
could lead you to find.

It is warm and it's safe.
It has a chair where I sit.
There is food in my fridge,
though only a tiny bit.

There is a lit fire.
Its glow is my light.
It is a place without fear,
a shield from the night.

It has a roof to protect,
keeps me dry from the rain.
It has a carpeted floor,
and no muddy stain.

This kingdom is mine,
though it is but a dream.
One I have often,
from my bed by the stream.

The

Dreamer

Lean on you

When my day seemed long and hard,
and my words got stuck in my head.
You knew just what to say.
You found my voice instead.

When my frustrations became too much.
My hands clenched into fists.
You always found the words,
the ones that others missed.

When my world becomes confusing
because something is out of place.
You make me look at you.
I enter my safe place.

When I can't understand myself.
I just don't know what to do.
I ask to be alone,
but then I lean on you.

A boy's Best Friend

This is my friend Eddy.
He never questions me.
It doesn't matter what I do,
he never leaves me be.

Sometimes he sits and stares.
He never says a word,
He never leaves my side.
He knows if I get scared.

He doesn't ask for anything.
He just likes food and his walk.
He is always happy to see me,
even if I hardly talk.

Eddy is not just a dog.
He is everything to me.
He is my Brother and my best friend,
a big part of our Family.

What about the boy

You look and see the man,
but what about the boy?
I was not given any love,
or even a small toy.

You look and see my clothes,
I wore them as a child.
I got them from an uncle,
he left them then just smiled.

You look and see I am tall,
I should know better now.
I had no one to teach me,
no one to show me how.

You look and I see you.
I no longer care what you think.
All I want is food,
and then to have a drink.

You look and see my home,
because this is where I live.
Relying on charity from others,
and all that they can give.

You look and see the man,
but I am still the boy that's lost.
Be grateful you know love,
because for me it had a cost.

The Crown

I bought you a pretty crown.
I laid it on your head.
No Mother looked more beautiful,
resting in her bed.

I had a silent whisper.
A smile and a runaway tear.
I thought of all Christmas past,
the ones when you were here.

This is the here and now,
and those were yesteryear...
I am glad of all my memories,
from times we got to share.

Wear your crown sweet lady.
Shine on Christmas day.
Gather all of the Angels,
and head them all this way.

Show them all their legacies
as they stand at heaven's door.
Catch the kisses, and feel the love,
that you left forever more.

Moving Mountains

I would move a mountain
if I thought you were behind.
To see your face again,
to make the years rewind.

I would find the strength
if I knew that you were there.
To chat like we once did,
with a coffee and a cake to share.

I would move a mountain,
as I shout out your name,
because since you went away,
things haven't been the same.

I tried to move a mountain.
It was far too heavy for me,
so instead I shall sit beside it,
as I relive each memory.

When life

becomes

too much

When life becomes too much,
and days seem hard to bear.
You keep running to that hole,
but I still find you there.

I will come and get you.
I will try to help you out.
I will never go away.
Even when you shout.

When the darkness falls,
I will still be here.
With every creeping shadow,
I will mask my fear.

Hide for how long is needed
until you can breathe again.
Just know that someone loves you,
it will help to ease the pain.

Don't rock the Boat

At times when steering my boat,
I find it rocks side to side.
I can't control the wheel,
so I run away and hide.

Then I feel the Thrashing.
It goes against the waves.
I want to cry out loud,
in the hope that someone saves.

Still, I keep on hiding,
whilst the voices in my head,
are arguing with each other,
and I can't hear what they said.

The waves turn into storms.
The day turns into night.
My boat which was my haven
has now become my fight.

It is then I wished I had spoken,
turned to that one friend,
asked someone to take the wheel,
someone's hand to lend.

A friend to help to steer
until the waves calmed down.
A friend for me to cling to,
so I wouldn't drown.

They are all around us.
They could have saved my boat,
if I had just reached out,
they would helped me stay afloat.

A mother's Love

When a Mother's legs become weary,
her load too much to bear.
Her child will still be priority,
as she gives up the only chair.

Though she is tired and worn.
She will listen to your woes.
She loves every inch of her babies,
from their heads to their toes.

She will give them all she has.
Use her last breath to say "I love you".
A Mother's love is in her blood.
It's a love forever true.

So when you see your Mother,
tell her how much you care,
and if her eyes look tired,
then tell her to take the chair.

The Gift of Christmas

Children are the gift of Christmas,
all wrapped up in love.

Tied up with a big heartstring.
A gift from up above.

They are the colouring books.
The chocolate selection box,

the Christmas Eve pyjamas,
and of course the warm bed socks.

Children are the smiling faces,
they are the laughter's sound.

They are the cosy fireplace,
they are the joy to be around

They light up a dark grey sky.
They are the games we play.

They are all the shining glitter.
They are the future of today.

Children are the magic.
The memories around the tree

Children are the gift of Christmas,
for us to love wholeheartedly.

I picked you a flower today,
though in a moment you will forget.
I'll pick you another tomorrow,
your memory will then rest.

I noticed when I gave you it,
there was a twinkle in your eye.
I knew that in that moment,
you remembered you and I.

That old familiar face,
the one that I made smile.
Reliving a special moment,
for just a little while.

Flower
of
Remembrance

.Did you recognise the flower?
It had a familiar scent.
Did it take you back?
To a time when something meant?

A Grandad and his great Granddaughter.
A Mother and a Son.
Dementia has no mercy,
when it shoots its gun.

Someone will always remember,
everything that you forget,
because treasured memories were made,
with everyone you met.

I stole nana's heart

I stole My Nana's heart.
She said she didn't mind.
She told me to keep it safe.
Where no one else would find.

So I put it in my mouth.
I chewed it very slow.
I knew that when I swallowed,
it would know where to go.

It would find its way to mine.
Grow big and whole again,
because a Nana's love,
runs through every vein.

It is always full of warmth.
Brings me so much joy.
It has so much to give,
for every girl and boy.

Nana's heart and mine,
now beat together as one,
so when she is not with me,
I know she still lives on.

From one mum to Another

I never signed a contract,
no instructions for me to read.
All I was given was a feeling,
from which I learnt to feed.

It taught me how to love.
It showed me how to care.
I see that I was empty,
until I felt you there.

'Salivary kiss'

I realised sleepless nights,
were something I would miss.
You taught me the value,
of a very salivary kiss.

No book could have prepared me,
for the years of Motherhood.
No words could have expressed,
or have made me understood.

'you opened my heart's door ♡'

Life was just a word,
until the day you came.
Then my world got bigger,
and the days were not the same.

Sometimes I sit and wonder,
could I have done something more.
Then I feel my heartbeat,
and the answer is just no.

Being a Mother has no rules.
There is no right or wrong.
It comes with no disguise.
It has a pull that is so strong.

It doesn't have an expiry date,
or a best before.
It began the very moment,
you opened my heart's door.

'no rules'

The Empty Space

They talk about the empty chair,
but they forget about that place.
The one that no one enters,
so it remains an empty space.

They talk about the empty chair,
it was once where you were sat.
What about the places though?
Where you were always at?

They talk about the empty chair,
not the life you left behind.
I search so many places,
in the hope that you I find.

They talk about the empty chair,
the one that I can't see.
What about the empty place?
That lives inside of me.

They talk about the empty chair,
they rock it to and fro.
There is no change in movement,
no matter where I go.

They talk about the empty chair,
they can not see that place.
The one where there is only I,
and the memory of your face.

Letter to Heaven

I sent a letter to heaven,
because I saw my Nana cry.
She told me it is where her Mammy lives,
she said it's in the sky.

I tried to phone her up first,
but it seems there's no one there.
I just wanted her to know,
that we all still care.

I hope that when she reads it,
she will come and play with me.
I hope Nana will stop crying,
and drinking lots of tea.

I didn't write her name on it.
I just addressed it to Above.
I then kissed the envelope,
before sealing it with love.

A Daddy and his Daughter

A Daddy and his Daughter,
two hearts entwined as one.
No matter how she grows,
his arms will still be strong.

He will always hold her,
hug her to his chest.
He will always promise,
that he will do his best.

A Daddy and his Daughter,
a love forever true.
The first man that she met
and will love her whole life through.

A Daddy and his little girl,
the way she will always stay.
He will always be there for her,
until his dying day.

Remembrance Day

Side by side we march. One by one we stand.
We are heavens soldiers. We once fought on this land.

We are all different ages. Some remain still young.
Their halos are the brightest. Their wings are perfectly hung.

God opens the pearly gates, On the 11th of November, and on
the 11th hour, we look on as you remember.

We stand and we salute you, for not forgetting what we've done.
We grace the clouds of heaven, knowing the battle was won.

We are not forgotten, though it was so long ago.
Our lives shall live forever, through those we did not know.

As you say lest we forget, we hold our heads up high.
We are heavens soldiers, marching in the sky.

Sisters

I appreciate I have a Sister,
and just how much she means.
We have had our stubborn moments,
yet also shared our dreams.

We have stood side by side,
although we are miles apart.
The blood that we both share,
connects us at the heart.

When the road seems long, and
you can't seem to see the end.
It is then that your Sister
is also your best friend.

Sisters walk together.
They hold one another's hand,
because when it really matters,
they will understand.

Dancing with Memories

When My days are over,
and I can not be seen.
Just look back on our photographs,
to places that we've been.
For no matter where I am,
or where it is you are.
I shall be somewhere watching,
either near or from afar.
You are my world and more.
You are every breath I take.
You are my every moment,
of every memory that I make.
So when the wind does blow,
and the sea calls out my name.
Just go back to that memory, and
relive it once again.

Look at me Nana

Look at me Nana,
Let me see your face.
Let me capture this memory
to put in my forever place.
Let me see those eyes,
that smile you save for me.
Let us turn this moment,
into a special memory.
One day I will grow tall, and
you will think that I've forgot,
but it's imprinted in my mind
to make sure that it is not.

Gay Pride

I saw you in the Schoolyard.
The wind blew on your face.
I didn't understand back then,
why my heart did race.

Years then passed me by.
Relationships came and went.
I didn't understand back then,
why others called me bent.

I tried hard to fit in with others,
at a cost to my true self.
Was I ashamed of who I was?
Scared of being left upon the shelf?

How could I face my Parents?
What would My Mother say?
Would my Dad be disappointed?
To know that I was gay.

That dreaded day arrived.
I knew I couldn't take any more.
I wanted to be me,
to stop hiding behind the door.

The moment that I came out,
felt like I was reborn.
Why did it take me so long?
Always feeling lost and torn.

Now I am a Somebody.
I no longer want to hide.
I am one of many,
and together we are GAYPRIDE.

The tapestry of Life

Many years ago,
a Tapestry was weaved.
It started with a petal,
then a rose was achieved.

The rose then blossomed,
one turned into two.
Flowers of pink were added,
and then the colour blue.

A garden with green grass.
A house in a little street.
Dandelions and daisies,
made it look so neat.

The tapestry then grew.
Weaved for many years.
That very first petal,
now had signs of tares.

Yet still, it held itself together,
hanging by a thread.
The rose that once blossomed,
was now fading instead.

The old becomes the new.
The new becomes the old.
The story of Family,
is the greatest story told.

Grandma's House

You won't remember the garden playhouse,
or the bikes that you were bought.
The lego bricks you played with,
or the treats that Nana brought.

You won't reminisce about pretty dresses,
or the shoes upon your feet.
You won't understand the importance.
Of all the people that you meet.

You won't think about your Grandparents,
for all the things they gave.
You are too busy collecting memories,
which in your heart you will save.

You will recall upon the fun times,
remember all the things we've done.
You will laugh at Nana's silliness,
and see then that it was fun.

You will think of Nana's house,
as the place you were free to roam,
and when you call upon those memories
you will be in your second home.

Home

When people think of home, they see a rooftop and a door.
For me it runs much deeper, home means so much more.

A rooftop holds no warmth if it protects a heart that's cold.
A door can lead to emptiness, or an evil can unfold.

Home comes from the heart, it can be found within a smile.
An umbrella can be a rooftop, it can go that extra mile.

Your eyes can be the doorway, to the view that people see.
Your hands can turn the handle, to a future you and me.

Let kindness be the fire, to warm a person's soul.
Let your words be the spade, to dig them from the hole.

Let generosity be the food, that helps them to grow strong.
Let laughter bring them the will, to want to carry on.

Home has many windows, each with a different view.
Some people only see, what you want them too.

I love being home to many, I am lucky in that way.
You too can be someone's roof, by being their home today.

thank you

Johnston Hale

PUBLICATIONS

If you would like to publish your own book or poetry collection, just write to us at johnston.hale@gmail.com with your submission or visit www.johnston-hale.co.uk

Printed in Great Britain
by Amazon

62f315d7-d1ec-428e-843e-0d38ab71c9b4R01